ALFR
BASIC ADULT
CHRISTMAS
PIANO BOOK
LEVEL ONE

FOREWORD

Those who devote time to learning to play the piano reap special rewards during the Christmas Season, when they find how much pleasure and satisfaction they can derive from playing some of their favorite carols. This can begin when the student is still in five-finger position, or in middle C position. To hear one's self playing the tunes that others have always had to provide, brings a realization that piano study really does offer special rewards. If the student has progressed to the point of playing harmonic intervals, three note chords, minor keys, etc., the rewards are proportionally greater, because music study is a thing that brings added pleasure with added progress.

With the above in mind, this book has been prepared for the use of students in ALFRED'S BASIC ADULT PIANO COURSE, Level 1. The pieces are arranged in graded order, and each one has a DUET PART playable at the same piano. Measures are numbered to make practicing the duets easier.

In the upper right corner of the first page of each piece, the student will see how these selections are correlated with Lesson Book 1. There are pieces here for everyone, and because Christmas carols provide special motivation, most students will find that they can play some of those that are a bit beyond their current level with just a little extra effort.

The authors wish to all who use and teach from this book a MERRY CHRISTMAS, and hope you will derive much pleasure from the music presented here.

CONTENTS

© Copyright MCMLXXXIV by Alfred Publishing Co., Inc.

Cover design: Linda Prendergast

Cover photography: James W. Franklin

Use after WARM-UP USING C, G⁷ & F CHORDS (page 29)
in ALFRED'S BASIC ADULT PIANO COURSE, Level 1.

JOLLY OLD SAINT NICHOLAS

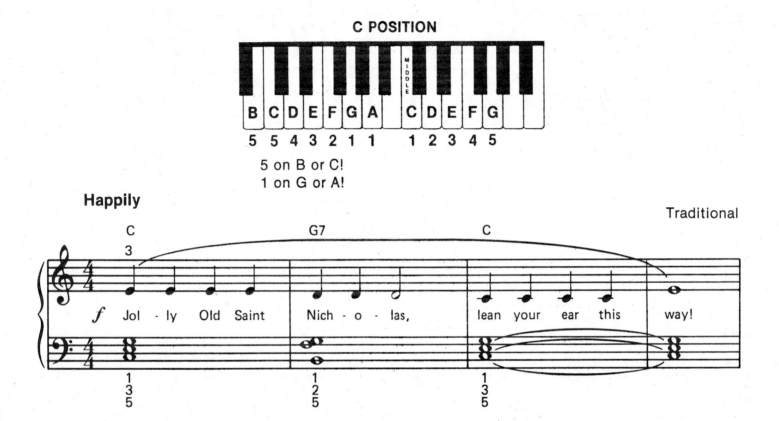

Happily

Traditional

DUET PART: (Student plays 1 octave higher.)

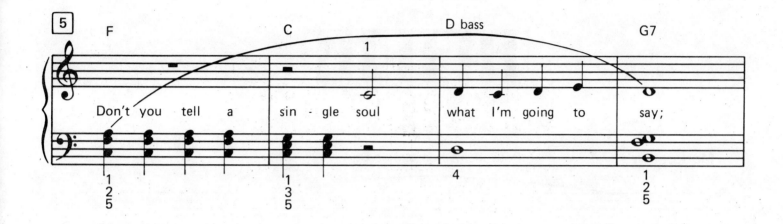

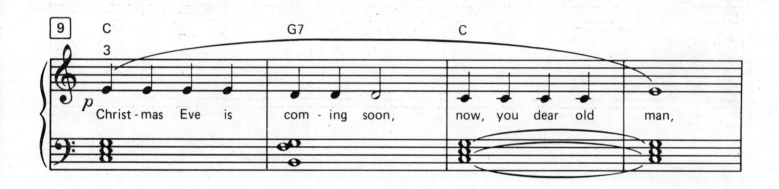

Use after MIDDLE C POSITION (page 42).

WE THREE KINGS OF ORIENT ARE

John Henry Hopkins

DUET PART: (Student plays 1 octave higher.)

5

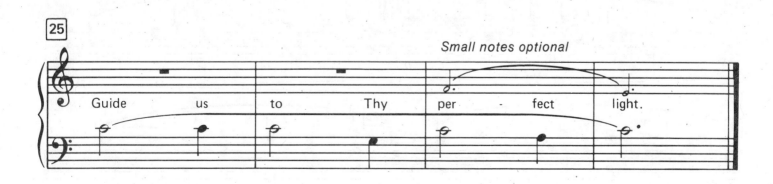

Small notes optional

6

IT CAME UPON THE MIDNIGHT CLEAR

MIDDLE C POSITION

DUET PART: (Student plays 1 octave higher.)

Use after HAPPY BIRTHDAY TO YOU! (page 45).

WE WISH YOU A MERRY CHRISTMAS

MIDDLE C POSITION

Traditional

DUET PART: (Student plays 1 octave higher.)

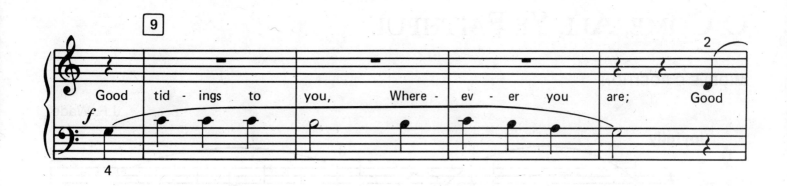

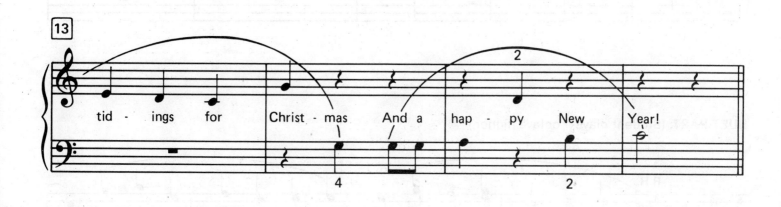

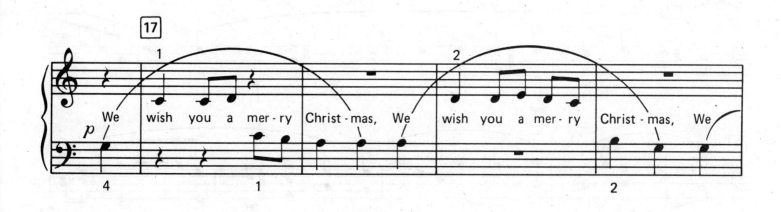

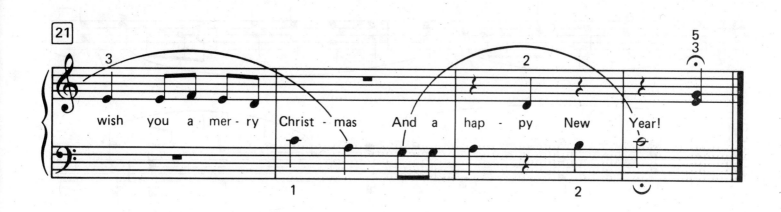

Use after INTRODUCING DOTTED QUARTER NOTES (page 48).

O Come, All Ye Faithful

MIDDLE C POSITION

J.F. Wade

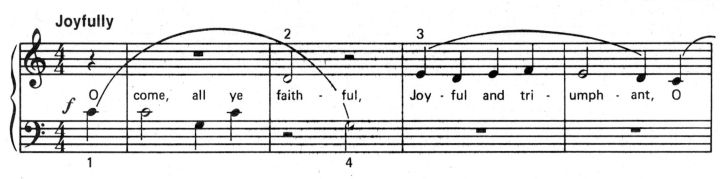

O come, all ye faith - ful, Joy - ful and tri - umph - ant, O

DUET PART: (Student plays 1 octave higher.)

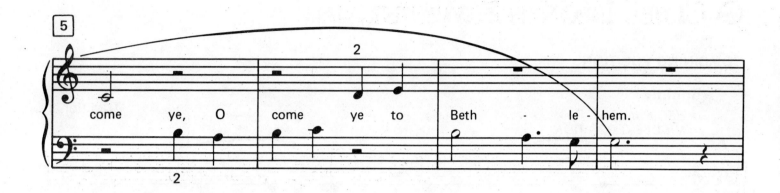

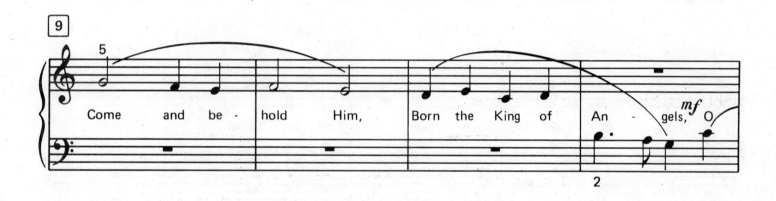

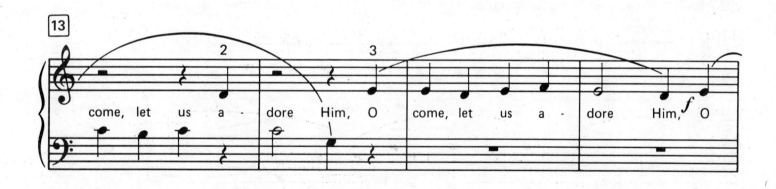

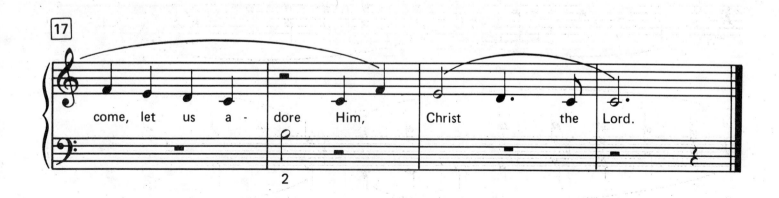

12

Use after INTRODUCING THE DOTTED QUARTER NOTE (page 48).

GO TELL IT ON THE MOUNTAIN

COMBINING POSITIONS

Brightly

Traditional

BEGIN IN MIDDLE C POSITION

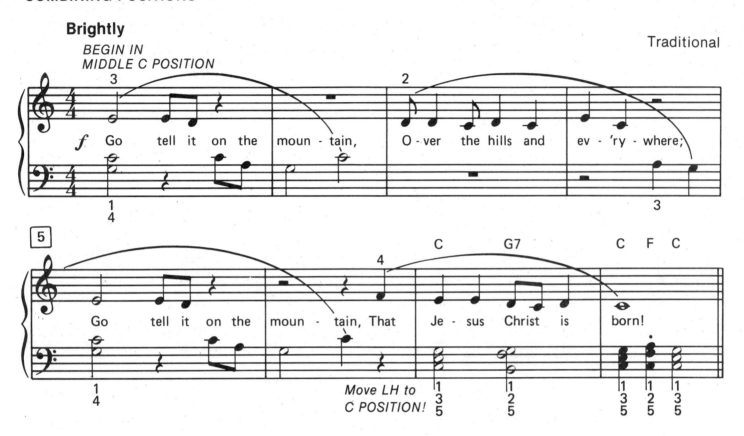

DUET PART: (Student plays 1 octave higher. Pairs of EIGHTH NOTES may be played long-short.)

D.C. al Fine

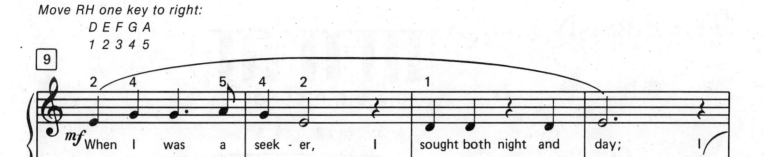

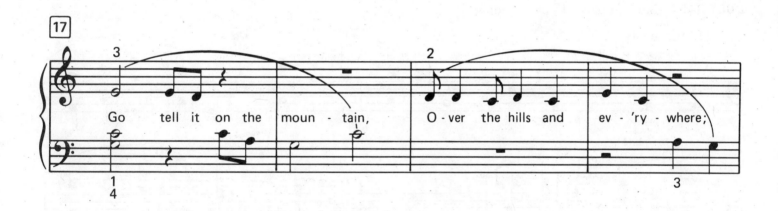

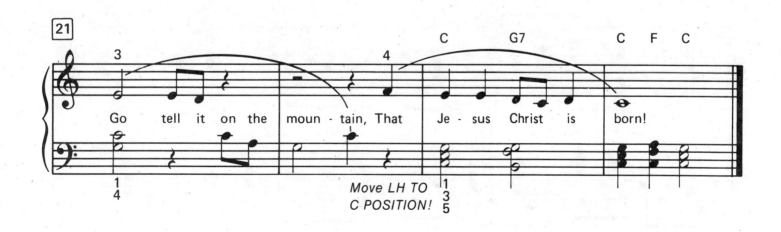

THE FIRST NOËL

Use after page 49.

MIDDLE C POSITION (WITH F♯)

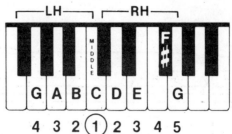

Traditional

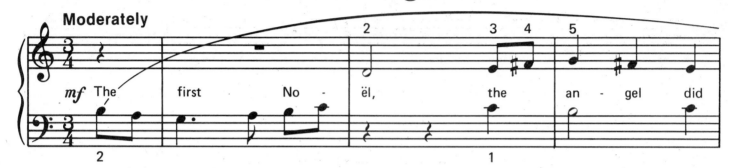

The first No - ël, the an - gel did

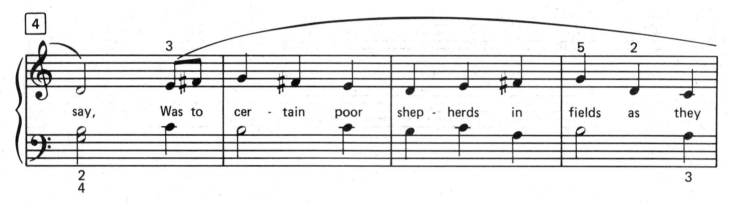

say, Was to cer - tain poor shep - herds in fields as they

DUET PART: (Student plays 1 octave higher.)

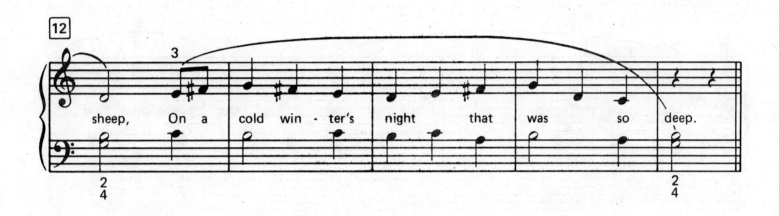

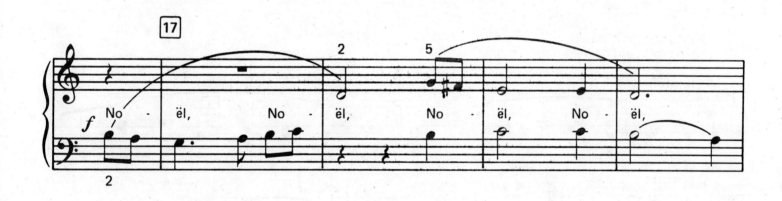

Use after MEASURING 6ths (page 52).

Up on the Housetop

C POSITION + 1

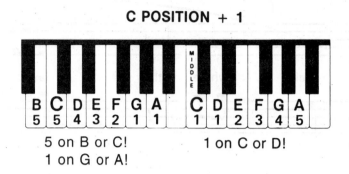

5 on B or C!
1 on G or A!

1 on C or D!

B.R. Hanby

Moderately fast

Up on the house - top rein - deer pause; Out jumps good old

DUET PART: (Student plays 1 octave higher.)

Moderately fast

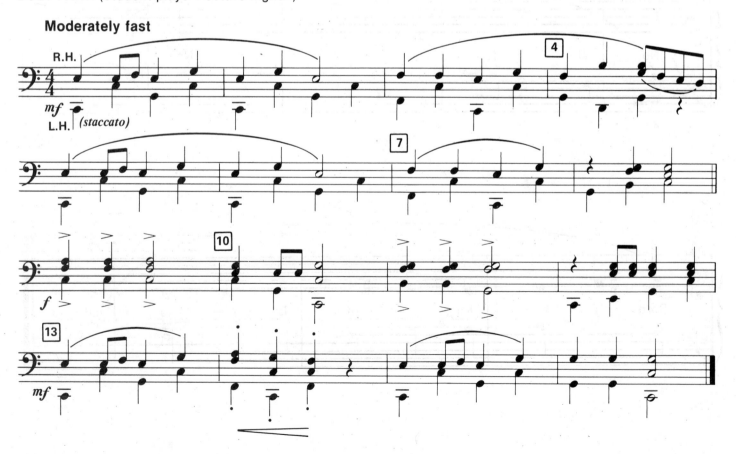

> ACCENT SIGN means play with special EMPHASIS!

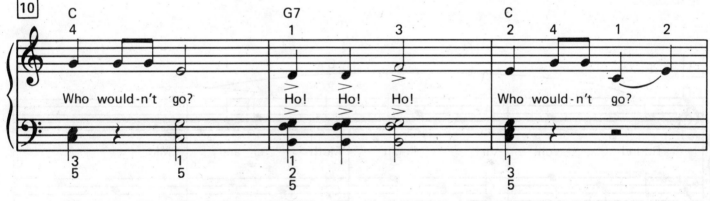

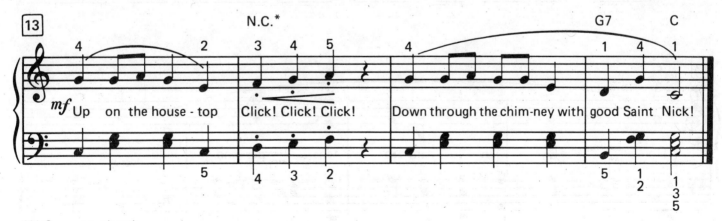

*N.C. = no chord.

Use after MEASURING 7ths & OCTAVES (page 58).

SILENT NIGHT

Moderately slow

Franz Gruber

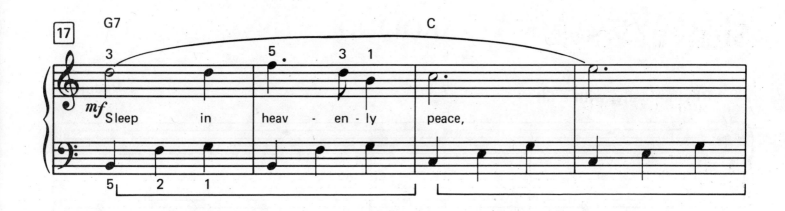

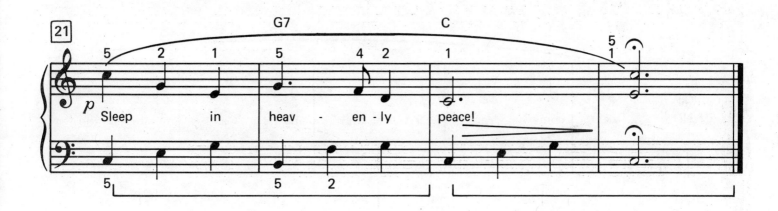

DUET PART:

Moderately slow

Play this part 8va throughout

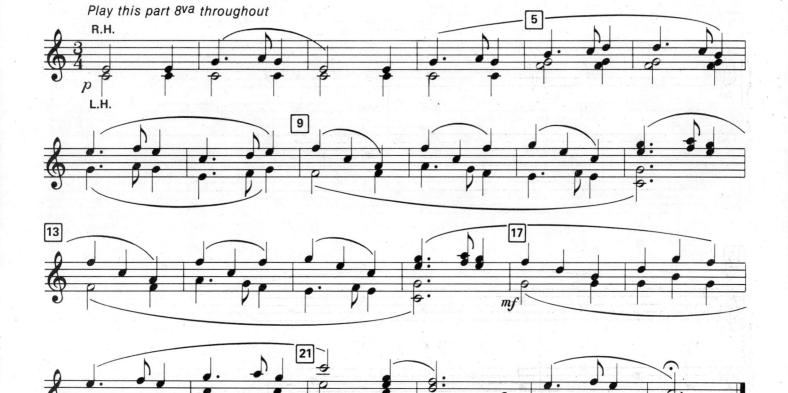

Use after THE MAJOR SCALE (page 62).

HERE WE COME A-CAROLING

Traditional

*a tempo = return to original tempo.

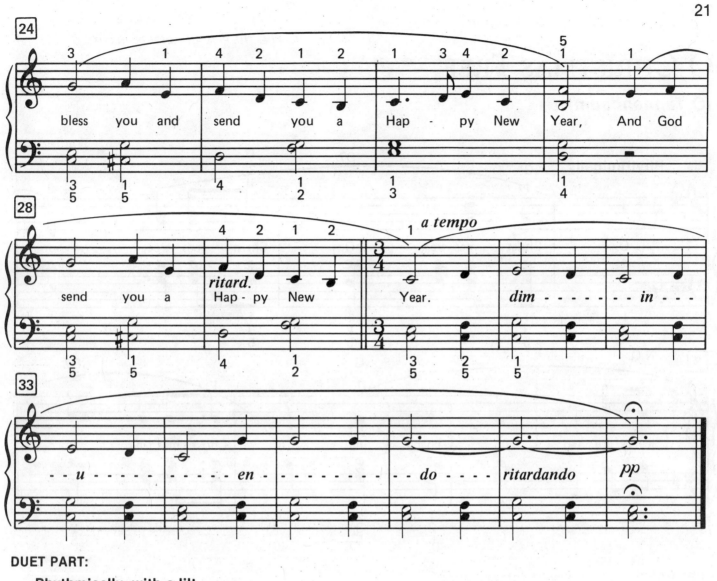

DUET PART:

Rhythmically, with a lilt

Play this part 8ᵛᵃ throughout

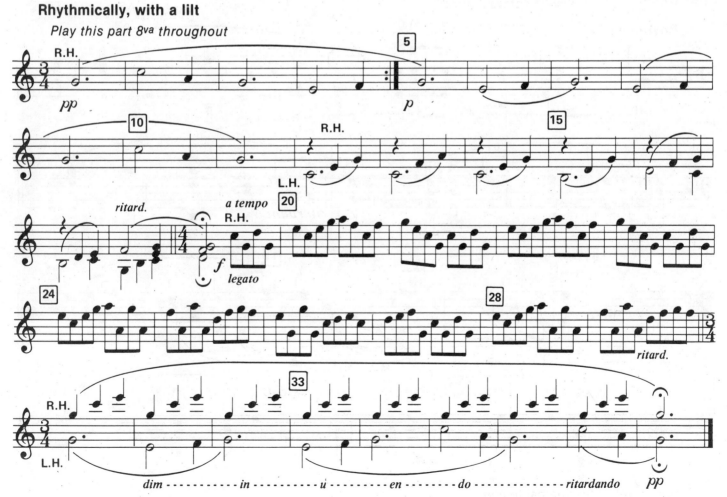

Use after THE PRIMARY CHORDS IN G MAJOR (page 72).

O CHRISTMAS TREE

(O Tannenbaum)

Traditional

DUET PART: (Student plays 1 octave higher.)

*The dotted rhythm may be taught by memory, or by rote, at this point.

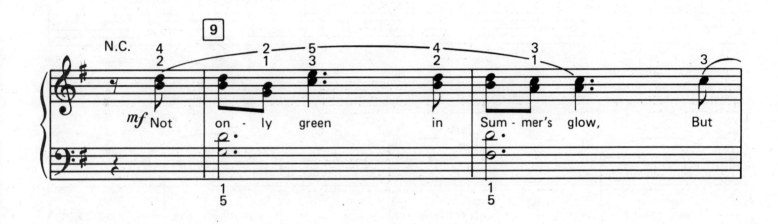

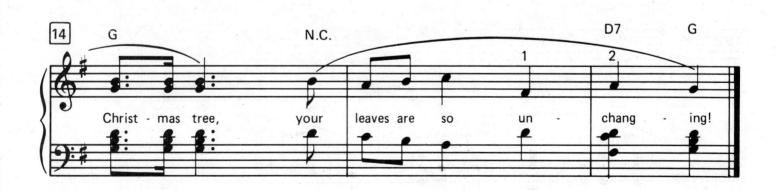

Use after LITTLE BROWN JUG (page 75).

Here's a very fancy arrangement, full of sleigh bells and laughter!

JINGLE BELLS

Moderately fast

James Pierpont

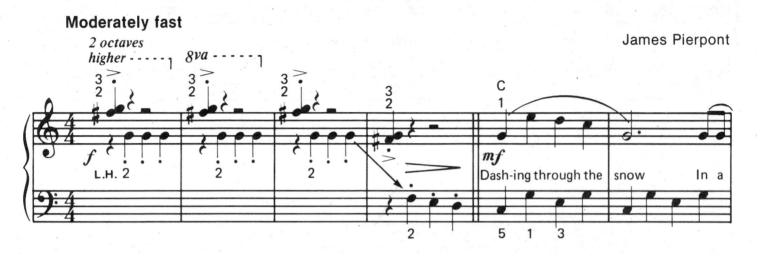

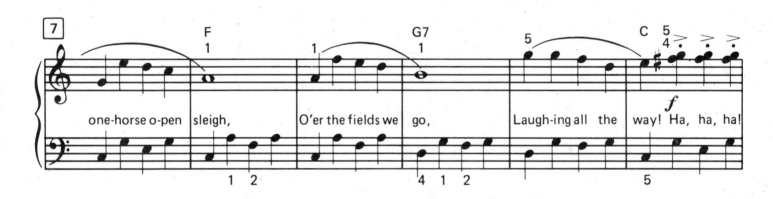

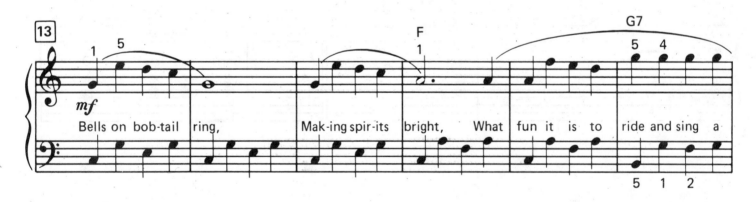

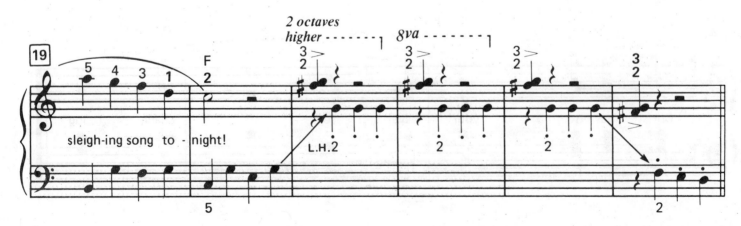